Grandparents:

A Book of
Favorite Quotations

D0170885

Grandparents:
A Book of
Favorite Quotations

Edited by Kristin Shea

BARNES
&NOBLE
BOOKS
NEW YORK

Compilation copyright © 2003 by Barnes & Noble, Inc.

2003 Barnes & Noble Books

ISBN 0-7607-4066-6

Printed and bound in the United States of America

M 9 8 7 6 5 4 3 2 1

I DECIDED THE OTHER DAY TO LOOK THROUGH A memory box filled with the cards that people sent me when I had my daughter. The same feeling came over me then as when the cards first started arriving. It is amazing to consider the overwhelming joy that such a small person can bring to the world without any knowledge whatsoever of that world. So imagine the particular joy of becoming a grandparent. Conventional wisdom tells us that being a grandparent is wonderful because one gets to do all the fun stuff of parenting without any of the disciplinary baggage.

As parents, we worry that each decision we make will affect the outcome of the future adult we are trying to mold. Grandparents do not suffer from this affliction: Buy your grandchild another ice cream cone, get the toy she's been begging for—spoiling is not a consideration. My mother could not believe her eyes when she arrived at her father's house to pick my sister and me up from an overnight visit and saw us sliding down the stairs on a roll-away bed mattress. Surely, if my mother had suggested such a thing as a child, my grandfather would have shot down the idea on the pretense of safety…but, in his mellower older years, he thought it was neat to listen to his granddaughters' wicked laughter as they flung themselves down the stairs.

What is it that allows a grandparent to just "be in the moment" with a grandchild? Could it be the general wisdom that comes with age, or is it the specific knowledge that your child is a competent adult, capable of raising his own child? Obviously, you must have been doing something right even though at the time it felt like you were making it up as you went along. The adage turns out to be true: We can't do any worse raising our own children than our parents did raising us. So sit back and relax, your granddaughter is going to turn out just as well, if not better than your daughter did. You've already agonized over the minutiae of parenting. Now's the time to enjoy the quirks of your grandchildren, without worrying about trying to tame them.

The Joys of
Grandparenting

A grandchild is a miracle, but a renewed relationship with your own children is even a greater one.

—T. BERRY BRAZELTON

The feeling of grandparents for their grandchildren can be expressed this way: "Our children are dear to us; but when we have grandchildren, they seem to be more dear than our children were".... It goes right back to those wishes that were made for them when they were little girls: the wish that they would live to become grandmothers someday. So when the time comes and they reach grandmotherhood, they do extra little duties to show their appreciation.

—HENRY OLD COYOTE, member of the Crow Nation

Heredity is a strong factor, even in architecture. Necessity first mothered invention. Now invention has little ones of her own, and they look just like grandma.

—E. B. WHITE

If becoming a grandmother was only a matter of choice, I should advise every one of you straight away to become one. There is no fun for old people like it!

—HANNAH WHITHALL SMITH

There are fathers who do not love their children; there is no grandfather who does not adore his grandson.

—VICTOR HUGO

Every generation revolts against its fathers and makes friends with his grandfathers.

—LEWIS MUMFORD

Few things are more delightful than grandchildren fighting over your lap.

—DOUG LARSON

The simplest toy, one which even the youngest child can operate, is called a grandparent.

—SAM LEVENSON

Nobody can do for little children what grandparents do. Grandparents sort of sprinkle stardust over the lives of little children.

—ALEX HALEY

Perfect love sometimes does not come till the first grandchild.

—WELSH PROVERB

Soon I will be an old, white-haired lady, into whose lap someone places a baby, saying, "Smile, Grandma!"—I, who myself so recently was photographed on my grandmother's lap.

—LIV ULLMANN

Outings are so much more fun when we can savor them through the children's eyes.

—LAWANA BLACKWELL

D'you call life a bad job? Never! We've had our ups and downs, we've had our struggles, we've always been poor, but it's been worth it, ay, worth it a hundred times I say when I look round at my children.

—W. SOMERSET MAUGHAM

Life's more amusing than we thought.

—ANDREW LANG

A baby is God's opinion that life should go on.

—CARL SANDBURG

Youth fades; love droops; the leaves of friendship fall; a mother's secret hope outlives them all!

—OLIVER WENDELL HOLMES

What feeling is so nice as a child's hand in yours?
So small, so soft and warm, like a kitten huddling
in the shelter of your clasp.

—Marjorie Holmes

A mother is not a person to lean on, but a person
to make leaning unnecessary.

—Dorothy Canfield Fisher

Children's children are a crown to the aged.

—Proverbs 17:6

The pairing of young and old creates an openness not always found in adult relationships.

—SUZANNE LARRONDE, photographer

Home is the place where, when you have to go there, they have to take you in.

—ROBERT FROST

Grandchildren are more tolerant of you than their parents are. Maybe it's because they have to put up with your foibles for a shorter span of time.

—CELESTINE SIBLEY

You don't choose your family. They are God's gift to you, as you are to them.

—DESMOND TUTU

Grandchildren provide us with some of our proudest occasions, some of our tenderest experiences, and, without question, some of our funniest moments.

—CATHARINE BRANDT

I am an onlooker on my daughter's dance, which I...made possible because she came through me...I'm not a part of her dance. Yet whenever she takes a pause and needs someone to talk to, I am there. But that special dance with the child and the future is hers.

—LIV ULLMANN

A child needs a grandma to spoil him a bit,
Someone with time on her hands who will sit
In an old-fashioned rocker that shivers and squeaks
And listen to words that a little boy speaks.

—EDNA JAQUES

Children are the only form of immortality that we
can be sure of.

—PETER USTINOV

In childhood days, dear Grandmother, it was you
Who taught me all of nature's loveliness.

—MAY ALLREAD BAKER

You are the sun, grandma, you are the sun in my life.

—KITTY TSUI, author, artist

Each memory revives some incident
Of early married life, of hardships shared,
Of children gathered round, of work and play,
Of little broken hopes by love repaired.

—INGA GILSON CALDWELL, poet, educator

A child's hand in yours—what tenderness it arouses, what power it conjures. You are instantly the very touchstone of wisdom and strength.

—MARJORIE HOLMES

The woman who creates and sustains a home, and under whose hands children grow up to be strong and pure men and women is a creator second only to God.

—HELEN HUNT JACKSON

There are so many things about
My childhood I cannot recall;
But of my grandma's house, it seems
That I remember all.

—JESSIE WILMORE MURTON

You are the bows from which your children as living arrows are sent forth.

—KAHLIL GILBRAN

She is cuddling the baby in Grandmother's
    rocker,
And singing an old-time song;
In this armchair my grandmother once rocked
    Mother,
Her arms, like her love, were strong;
And the dear little baby she used to hold
Is a woman now, with the long years told.

—ANNE CAMPBELL

The family is the first essential cell of human
society.

—POPE JOHN XXIII

I value this delicious home feeling as one of the
choicest gifts a parent can bestow.

—WASHINGTON IRVING

When I stopped seeing my mother with the eyes of a child, I saw the woman who helped me give birth to myself.

—NANCY FRIDAY

Grandma always made you feel she had been waiting to see just you all day and now the day was complete.

—MARCY DEMAREE

Grandma was the heart of this family. Her love and support were total and unconditional.

—MARCY DEMAREE

Call not that man wretched, who whatever ills he
suffers, has a child to love.

—ROBERT SOUTHEY, writer, poet

The reason grandparents and grandchildren get
along so well is that they have a common enemy.

—SAM LEVENSON

I am a breathing, ambulatory armchair
the perfect place for cuddles.

—PAM BROWN

It is as grandmothers that our mothers come into the fullness of their grace. When a man's mother holds his child in her gladdened arms he is aware of the roundness of life's cycle; of the mystic harmony of life's ways.

—CHRISTOPHER MORLEY

Grandparents are frequently more congenial with their grandchildren that with their children. An old man, having retired from active life, regains the gaiety and irresponsibility of childhood. He is ready to play.... He cannot run with his son, but he can totter with his grandson. Our first and last steps have the same rhythm; our first and last walks are similarly limited.

—ANDRÉ MAUROIS

The closest friends I have made all through life have been people who also grew up close to a loved and loving grandmother or grandfather.

—MARGARET MEAD

Wisdom &
Experience

Our grandparents used to say that we must eat a peck of dirt before we die, and they were right. And you must read a lot of rubbish before you die, as well, because an exclusive diet of master-pieces will give you spiritual dyspepsia. How do you know that a mountain peak is glorious if you have never scrambled through a dirty valley?

—ROBERTSON DAVIES

In my grandmother's house there was always
    chicken soup
And talk of the old country.

—LOUIS SIMPSON

One generation plants the trees; another gets the shade.

—CHINESE PROVERB

There are only two families in the world, my old grandmother used to say, the Haves and the Have-nots.

—Miguel de Cervantes

The hardest years in life are those between ten and seventy.

—Helen Hayes

Avoid providing material for the drama that is always stretched tight between parents and children; it uses up much of the children's strength and wastes the love of the elders, which acts and warms even if it doesn't comprehend.

—Rainer Maria Rilke

The moment a child is born, the mother is also born. She never existed before. The woman existed, but the mother, never. A mother is something absolutely new.

—Rajneesh

A mother never realizes that her children are no longer children.

—Holbrook Jackson

When I show my grandchildren, I have a wonderful feeling of pride. I say, "See that crane way, way up there? Grandma used to run a crane like that during the war."

—Jennette Hyman Nuttall

Age puzzles me. I thought it was a quiet time. My seventies were interesting and fairly serene, but my eighties are passionate. I grow more intense as I age.

—FLORIDA SCOTT-MAXWELL

Her grandmother, as she gets older, is not fading but rather becoming more concentrated.

—PAULETTE BATES ALDEN, writer, educator

If nothing is going well, call your grandmother.

—ITALIAN PROVERB

And in the end, it's not the years in your life that count. It's the life in your years.

—ABRAHAM LINCOLN

Age is something that doesn't matter, unless you are a cheese.

—Billie Burke

There are compensations for growing older. One is the realization that to be sporting isn't at all necessary. It is a great relief to reach this stage of wisdom.

—Cornelius Otis Skinner

No matter how old a mother is, she watches her middle-aged children for signs of improvement.

—Florida Scott-Maxwell

So much has been said and sung of beautiful young girls, why don't somebody wake up to the beauty of old women?

—HARRIET BEECHER STOWE

Age does not protect you from love, but love to some extent protects you from age.

—JEANNE MOREAU

Somewhere in the past
lie the roots to
a legacy of love,
of faith and hope
handed down through generations
of mothers.

—MARIANNE MILLER

The longer I live the more beautiful life becomes.

—FRANK LLOYD WRIGHT

In case you're worried about what's going to become of the younger generation, it's going to grow up and start worrying about the younger generation.

—ROGER ALLEN

By the time a man realizes that maybe his father was right, he usually has a son who thinks he's wrong.

—CHARLES WADSWORTH

If wrinkles must be written on our brows, let them not be written upon the heart. The spirit should never grow old.

—JAMES A. GARFIELD

At books, or work, or healthy play,
Let all my years be passed;
That I may give for every day
A good account at last.

—ISAAC WATTS

Men do not quit playing because they grow old; they grow old because they quit playing.

—OLIVER WENDELL HOLMES.

Your descendants shall gather your fruits.

—Virgil

As you are a seven, so you are at seventy.

—Jewish proverb

That which seems the height of absurdity in one generation often becomes the height of wisdom in another.

—Adlai Stevenson

All the time a person is a child he is both a child and learning to be a parent. After he becomes a parent he becomes predominantly a parent reliving childhood.

—Dr. Benjamin Spock

I shall feel no regret for roses which have faded with the passing of fleeting spring; I also love the grapes on the vine, which have ripened in bunches beneath the hill.

—ALEKSANDR PUSHKIN

She met the hardships
Of everyday life...
A pioneer mother
Making a priceless contribution
To the ages.

—BERNICE C. HEISLER

When you cease to make a contribution, you begin to die.

—ELEANOR ROOSEVELT

If you want good advice, consult an old man.

—ROMANIAN PROVERB

Surviving is important, but thriving is elegant.

—MAYA ANGELOU

Youth fades; love droops, the leaves of friendship fall; a mother's secret hope outlives them all.

—OLIVER WENDELL HOLMES

He who would pass his declining years with honor and comfort, should, when young, consider that he may one day become old, and remember when he is old, that he has once been young.

—JOSEPH ADDISON

I grasped her hand like a common consoling friend and felt, immediately, the grim forbidding strength of her, undiminished all these years.

—LOUISE ERDRICH

I am rich with years, a millionaire! I have been part of my own generation, then I watched my children's generation grow up, then my grand-children's and now my great-grandchildren's.

—DOLORES GARCIA

Life is the only real counselor; wisdom unfiltered through personal experience does not become a part of the moral tissue.

—EDITH WHARTON

We turn not older with years, but newer every day.

—EMILY DICKINSON

They draw me to them: women who have grown
Wise with the wisdom that right living brings.
Old mothers who have suffered and have known
A triumph over many conquered things...

—GRACE NOLL CROWELL

To keep the heart unwrinkled, to be hopeful, kindly, cheerful, reverent that is to triumph over old age.

—AMOS BRONSON ALCOTT, writer, philosopher

In old age we are like a batch of letters that some-one has sent. We are no longer in the past, we have arrived.

—Knut Hamsun

Ain't nobody going to censor me, no, sir! I'm a hundred and one years old, and at my age, honey, I can say what I want!

—Annie Elizabeth Delany

Even if I knew that tomorrow the world would go to pieces, I would still plant my apple tree.

—Dr. Martin Luther King, Jr.

To become a grandmother is to be suddenly piercingly aware of the brevity of human life.

—CHARLOTTE GRAY

Grandparents are to be thanked
for changing a child's fear of old age
into a thing of strange beauty.

—CHARLES AND ANN MORSE

Have courage for the great sorrows of life and patience for the small ones; and when you have laboriously accomplished your daily task, go to sleep in peace.

—VICTOR HUGO

Life is no brief candle to me. It is a sort of splendid torch which I have got hold of for the moment, and I want to make it burn as brightly as possible before handing it on to future generations.

—GEORGE BERNARD SHAW

As a white candle in a holy place,
So is the beauty of an aged face.

—JOSEPH CAMPBELL

I long to put the experience of fifty years at once into your young lives, to give you at once the key of that treasure chamber every gem of which has cost me tears and struggles and prayer, but you must work for these inward treasures yourself.

—HARRIET BEECHER STOWE

The greatest use of life is to spend it for something that will outlast it.

—WILLIAM JAMES

Once your children are grown up and have children of their own, the problems are theirs, and the less the older generation interferes the better.

—ELEANOR ROOSEVELT

So many things we love are you, I can't seem to explain except by little things, by flowers and beautiful handmade things—small stitches. So much of our reading and thinking—so many sweet customs and so much of our...well, our religion. It is all *you*. I hadn't realized it before. This is so vague but do you see a little, dear Grandma? I want to thank you.

—ANNE MORROW LINDBERGH

Lessons for Our Grandchildren

Being considerate of others will take you and your children further in life than any college or professional degree.

—MARIAN WRIGHT EDELMAN

You've got to do your own growing, no matter how tall your grandfather was.

—IRISH PROVERB

Besides the noble art of getting things done, there is nobler art of leaving things undone. The wisdom of life consists in the elimination of nonessentials.

—LIN YUTANG

Not a tenth of us who are in business are doing as well as we could if we merely followed the principles that were known to our grandfathers.

—William Feather

It's one of nature's ways that we often feel closer to distant generations than to the generation immediately preceding us.

—Igor Stravinsky

I think a lot of our problems are because people don't listen to our children. It is not always easy. They're not always so brilliant that you want to spend hours with them. But it is very important to listen to them.

—Barbara Bush

Our children are not going to be just "our children"—they are going to be other people's husbands and wives and the parents of our grandchildren.

—MARY S. CALDERONE

To hold the same views at forty as we held at twenty is to have been stupefied for a score of years, and take rank, not as a prophet, but as an unteachable brat, well birched and none the wiser.

—ROBERT LOUIS STEVENSON

Treat people as if they were what they ought to be and you help them to become what they are capable of being.

—JOHANN W. VON GOETHE

A conservative is someone who makes no changes and consults his grandmother when in doubt.

—Woodrow Wilson

You must learn day by day, year by year, to broaden your horizon. The more things you love, the more you are interested in, the more you enjoy, the more you are indignant about, the more you have left when anything happens.

—Ethel Barrymore

Experience is simply the name we give our mistakes.

—Oscar Wilde

He that gives good advice, builds with one hand; he that gives good counsel and example, builds with both; but he that gives good admonition and bad example, builds with one hand and pulls down with the other.

—FRANCIS BACON

If you can learn from hard knocks, you can also learn from soft touches.

—CAROLYN KENMORE, author, model

They may forget what you said, but they will never forget how you made them feel.

—CARL W. BUECHNER

Be gentle with the young.

—JUVENAL

You are the living link to the past. Tell your grandchildren the story of the struggles waged, at home and abroad; of sacrifices freely made for freedom's sake.

—GEORGE H. W. BUSH

Stop thinking your grandchildren will be OK no matter how wasteful or destructive you may be, since they can go to a nice new planet on a spaceship.

—KURT VONNEGUT

It is the malady of our age that the young are so busy teaching us that they have no time left to learn.

—Eric Hoffer

When a father gives to his son, both laugh; when a son gives to his father, both cry.

—Jewish proverb

Let us be grateful to people who make us happy; they are the charming gardeners who make our souls blossom.

—Marcel Proust

The best portion of a good man's life is his little, nameless, unremembered acts of kindness and of love.

—William Wordsworth

You might as well fall flat on your face as lean over too far backwards.

—James Thurber

Nobody can make you feel inferior without your permission.

—Eleanor Roosevelt

What monstrous absurdities and paradoxes have resisted whole batteries of serious arguments, and then crumbled swiftly into dust before the ringing death-knell of a laugh!

—AGNES REPPLIER

If you have knowledge, let others light their candles in it.

—MARGARET FULLER

Children require guidance and sympathy far more than instruction.

—ANNE SULLIVAN

If a child is to keep alive his inborn sense of wonder…he needs the companionship of at least one adult who can share it, rediscovering with him the joy, excitement, and mystery of the world we live in.

—RACHEL CARSON

It's so important to give your children and grand-children inspiration…. Teach them to notice, to pay attention, to appreciate, and to be inquisitive. Don't just look, try to see.

—IRINA BARONOVA-TENNANT

For finally, we are as we love. It is love that meas-ures our stature.

—WILLIAM SLOANE COFFIN

The art of being wise is the art of knowing what to overlook.

—WILLIAM JAMES

The righteous man leads a blameless life; blessed are his children after him.

—PROVERBS 20:7

Beware how you take away hope from another human being.

—OLIVER WENDELL HOLMES

Grandchildren graze, like deer, on the long gray hair of their grandparents; that is their wisdom.

—TAUTACHCHO, member of the Chumash people

Remember this—that very little is needed to make a happy life

—MARCUS AURELIUS

Self-pity gets you nowhere. One must have the adventurous daring to accept oneself as a bundle of possibilities and undertake the most interesting game in the world—making the most of one's best.

—RICHARD WILLARD ARMOUR, historian

A good man leaves an inheritance for his children's children.

—PROVERBS 13:22

What lies behind us and what lies before us are tiny matters compared to what lies within us.

—OLIVER WENDELL HOLMES

It is better to know some of the questions than all of the answers.

—JAMES THURBER

Three grand essentials to happiness in this life are something to do, something to love, and something to hope for.

—attributed to JOSEPH ADDISON

Treat the earth well: it was not given to you by your parents, it was loaned to you by your children. We do not inherit the earth from our ancestors, we borrow it from our children.

—Native-American proverb

A passionate interest in what you do is the secret of long life, whether it is helping old people or children or making cheese or growing earthworms.

—Julia Child

Where your pleasure is, there is your treasure: where your treasure, there your heart; where your heart, there your happiness.

—Saint Augustine

You are forgiven for your happiness and your successes only if you generously consent to share them.

—WILLIAM BLAKE

The strength of my conscience came from Grandma, who meant what she said. Perhaps nothing is more valuable for a child than living with an adult who is firm and loving—and Grandma was loving.

—MARGARET MEAD

My grandfather once told me that there are two kinds of people: those who work and those who take the credit. He told me to try to be in the first group; there was less competition there.

—INDIRA GANDHI

To our grandchildren, what we tell them about their parent's childhood and our own young years is living history.

−RUTH GOODE

We can do no great things; only small things with great love.

−MOTHER THERESA

Children are likely to live up to what you believe in them.

−LADY BIRD JOHNSON

I don't know who my grandfather was; I am much more concerned to know what his grandson will be.

—ABRAHAM LINCOLN

Lessons From
Our Grandchildren

Our grandchildren accept us for ourselves, without rebuke or effort to change us, as no one in
our entire lives has ever done, not our parents,
siblings, spouses, friends—and hardly ever our
own grown children.

—RUTH GOODE

Every child comes with the message that God is
not yet discouraged of man.

—RABINDRANATH TAGORE

Reasoning with a child is fine, if you can reach the
child's reason without destroying your own.

—JOHN MASON BROWN

I like to listen. I have learned a great deal from listening carefully. Most people never listen.

—ERNEST HEMINGWAY

A torn jacket is soon mended; but hard words bruise the heart of a child.

—HENRY WADSWORTH LONGFELLOW

That children link us with the future is hardly news.... When we participate in the growth of children, a sense of wonder must take hold of us, providing for us a sense of future.

—GRETA HOFMANN NEMIROFF

Only her mirror remained in the house.... And I, her pale granddaughter, who do not resemble her, look into it today as if into a lake that hides its treasures beneath the water.

—Lea Goldberg

When the voices of children are heard on the green
And whisp'rings in the dale;
The days of my youth rise fresh in my mind...

—William Blake

Every child is an artist. The problem is how to remain an artist once we grow up.

—Pablo Picasso

Sometimes it is a great joy just to listen to someone we love talking.

—Vincent McNabb, priest, writer

Grandparents and grandchildren have much to tell each other. One has just come from the spirit world and the other is on his way to the spirit world.

—Tautachcho, member of the Chumash People

Give a little love to a child and you get a great deal back.

—John Ruskin

Our patience will achieve more than our force.

—Edmund Burke

Of all nature's gifts to the human race, what is sweeter to a man than his children?

—Marcus Tullius Cicero

Children love to be alone because alone is where they know themselves, and where they dream.

—Roger Rosenblatt, journalist

The image of my grandmother, with whom I spent most of my time, fills the memories of my childhood.... She was always warm, open, and understanding toward me and tolerated mischief that not even my very patient mother would let me get away with.

—Emilie Schindler, Oskar Schindler's wife

Pretty much all the honest truth-telling there is in the world is done by children.

—Oliver Wendell Holmes

To laugh often and much; to win the respect of intelligent people and the affection of children; to earn the appreciation of honest critics and endure the betrayal of false friends; to appreciate beauty, to find the best in others; to leave the world a little better; whether by a healthy child, a garden patch or a redeemed social condition; to know even one life has breathed easier because you have lived. This is the meaning of success.

—Ralph Waldo Emerson

Things are new even at the age when we are supposed to have seen everything.

—Louise Erdrich

Acting childish seems to come naturally, but acting like an adult, no matter how old we are, just doesn't come easy to us.

—LILY TOMLIN

All grown-ups were once children, though few of them remember it.

—ANTOINE DE SAINT EXUPERY

The darling mispronunciations of childhood!– dear me, there's no music that can touch it; and how one grieves when it wastes away and dissolves into correctness, knowing it will never visit his bereaved ear again.

—MARK TWAIN

A new baby is like the beginning of all things—wonder, hope, a dream of possibilities. In a world that is cutting down its trees to build highways, losing its earth to concrete ... babies are almost the only remaining link with nature, with the natural world of living things from which we spring.

—Eda Le Shan

My very first feeling on looking at my grandson's face took me aback. It was as if neither of us were present, as if I for a second lost myself and couldn't find him in some ineffable void... As I came to, my first articulated feeling was actually one of respect for him.

—Anne Truitt, artist

The most useful and interesting letters we get here from home are from children seven or eight years old.... They write simply and naturally, and without straining for effect. They tell all they know, and then stop.

—MARK TWAIN

Peculiar isn't it?.... First you're scolding your children, and then all at once they're so smart they're scolding *you*.

—ANNE TYLER

None are so old as those who have outlived enthusiasm.

—HENRY DAVID THOREAU

In the effort to give good and comforting answers to the young questioners whom we love, we very often arrive at good and comforting answers for ourselves.

—RUTH GOODE

The person who can bring the spirit of laughter into a room is indeed blessed.

—BENNETT A. CERF

Holding these babies in my arms makes me realize the miracle my husband and I began.

—BETTY FORD

To speak truly, few adult persons can see nature...
The sun illuminates only the eye of the man, but
shines into the eye and heart of the child.

—RALPH WALDO EMERSON

Against the assault of laughter, nothing can stand.

—MARK TWAIN

Children are a wonderful gift.... They have an
extraordinary capacity to see into the heart of
things and to expose sham and humbug for
what they are.

—DESMOND TUTU

Children are curious and are risk takers. They have lots of courage. They venture out into a world that is immense and dangerous. A child initially trusts life and the processes of life.

—JOHN BRADSHAW, author, psychologist

The soul is healed by being with children.

—FYODOR DOSTOEVSKY

What is most appealing about young folks, after all, is the changes, not the still photograph of finished character but the movie, the soul in flux.

—THOMAS PYNCHON

A grandchild challenges the grandparent
to put aside all that stuff
and have fun.

—CHARLES AND ANN MORSE

She brings nice goodies
does my Gran

—PAM BROWN

Laughing at Ourselves

A mother becomes a true grandmother the day she stops noticing the terrible things her children do because she is so enchanted with the wonderful things her grandchildren do.

—LOIS WYSE

Wrinkles should merely indicate where the smiles have been.

—MARK TWAIN

While grandma looks forward to special moments with her grandchild, she must now schedule those moments in between her other engagements, like working, working out, and being worked over (nails and hair).

—PAULA LINDEN AND SUSAN GROSS

My grandmother died before tea bags. I am grateful.
My mother never admitted their existence.

—M. F. K. FISHER

How stunning are the changes which age makes
in a man while he sleeps!

—MARK TWAIN

Why do grandparents and grandchildren get along
so well? They have the same enemy—the mother.

—CLAUDETTE COLBERT

Does Grandpa love to baby-sit his grandchildren? Are you kidding? By day he is too busy taking hormone shots at the doctor's or chip shots on the golf course. At night he and Grandma are too busy doing the cha-cha.

—HAL BOYLE

Never have children, only grandchildren.

—GORE VIDAL

Life would be infinitely happier if we could only be born at the age of eighty and gradually approach eighteen.

—MARK TWAIN

They say genes skip generations. Maybe that's why grandparents find their grandchildren so likable.

—JOAN MCINTOSH

A grandmother pretends she doesn't know who you are on Halloween.

—ERMA BOMBECK

Have children while your parents are still young enough to take care of them.

—RITA RUDNER

Your sons weren't made to like you. That's what grandchildren are for.

—JANE SMILEY

No cowboy was ever faster on the draw than a grandparent pulling a baby picture out of a wallet.

—ANONYMOUS

I have found the best way to give advice to your children is to find out what they want and then advise them to do it.

—HARRY S TRUMAN

By the time the youngest children have learned to keep the house tidy, the oldest grandchildren are on hand to tear it to pieces.

—CHRISTOPHER MORLEY

If you can't make it better, you can laugh at it.

—ERMA BOMBECK

Reasoning with a child is fine if you can reach the child's reason before losing your own.

—JOHN MASON BROWN, literary critic

I have had enough experience in all my years, and have read enough of the past, to know that advice to grandchildren is usually wasted.

—HARRY S TRUMAN

I was watching the Super Bowl with my ninety-two-year-old grandfather, and our team scored a touchdown. When they showed the instant replay, he thought they scored another one. I was going to tell him, but I figured the game he was watching was better.

—STEPHEN WRIGHT, comedian

My grandmother started walking five miles a day when she was sixty. She's ninety-seven now, and we don't know where the hell she is.

—ELLEN DEGENERIS

A chimney smokes; a dog barks; a grandparent baby-sits.

—EDWINA SHERUDI, author

I don't want to *fight* old age, but I'm not about to invite it to live in, either. I want a nice symbiotic relationship with it, where we are totally unaware of each other.

—BETTY WHITE

Children are a great comfort in your old age—and they help you reach it faster, too.

—LIONEL KAUFFMAN

The big-city Grandpa has gone big time.... He is the life of every party, and out to prove he is just as young as he ever was.

—HAL BOYLE

Always be nice to your children because they are the ones who will choose your rest home.

—Phyllis Diller

Laughter is one of the very privileges of reason, being confined to the human species.

—Thomas Carlyle

The first half of our lives is ruined by our parents, and the second half by our children.

—Clarence Darrow

Inside every older person is a younger person—wondering what the hell happened.

—Cora Harvey Armstrong

Elephants and grandchildren never forget.

—ANDY ROONEY

I was young and foolish then; now I am old and foolisher.

—MARK TWAIN